Look for the Blessing

Orlando Ceaser

Look for the Blessing

Orlando Ceaser

Belleville, Ontario, Canada

Look for the Blessing
Copyright © 2003, Orlando Ceaser

National Library of Canada Cataloguing in Publication

Ceaser, Orlando, 1951-
    Look for the blessing / Orlando Ceaser.

ISBN 1-55306-586-7

    1. Christian poetry, American. I. Title.
PS3552.E32L66 2003   811'.6   C2003-902420-2

LSI Edition: 1-55306-588-3

**For more information or
to order additional copies, please contact:**

Orlando Ceaser
5 Gregory Lane
South Barrington, IL
60010 USA
oceaser@aol.com

Essence Publishing is a Christian Book Publisher dedicated to furthering the work of Christ through the written word. *Guardian Books* is an imprint of *Essence Publishing*. For more information, contact: 20 Hanna Court, Belleville, Ontario, Canada K8P 5J2. **Phone:** 1-800-238-6376. **Fax**: (613) 962-3055.**E-mail**: publishing@essencegroup.com **Internet**: www.essencegroup.com

Printed in Canada
by

Guardian
B O O K S

*To my parents, Ruby L. Ceaser and Norrell Ceaser,
for their unconditional love and unwavering belief
in me and God's purpose for my life.*

$\mathcal{T}$able of Contents

Preface

We expect the worst. We are suspicious, constantly in search of ulterior motives to explain acts of kindness. Our responses are the culmination of years of conditioning. We embrace Murphy's Law: "If anything can go wrong, it will go wrong." We say this even when things are going well. Negative expectations are a defense mechanism, a shield. We unconsciously fortify our frail egos against an anticipated run of bad luck by predicting trouble. When bad circumstances arrive, we say "I told you so," as if clairvoyant. On cue, we react badly to trouble by complaining, being disrespectful of others and taking out our frustrations on innocent bystanders. We should find an antidote to negativity and look for the blessings.

One day, I was waiting to take a flight from Philadelphia to Chicago. I rushed to the airport and discovered the flight was delayed. The 5:30 p.m. flight was scheduled to allegedly leave at 8:10 p.m. Bad weather in Chicago was listed as the reason for the delay. I checked into the airport club and was told by the agent that she would call me if the status of the flight changed. I went to the business section and reviewed my e-mail. After a while, I noticed the crowd dwindling, but did not become suspicious until I was virtually alone. I checked the airport monitor and noticed the flight time was changed to 6:15 p.m. It was exactly 6:10 p.m. I gathered my materials and inquired at the front desk of the airport club and asked if the monitor was correct. She replied that it was and said that the plane was about to take off. I asked about the other ticket agent who promised to notify me if the status changed and was told she had left for the evening.

I ran to the gate and arrived just as the plane was pulling away. I explained my situation to the gate agent, but there was nothing she could do. I was momentarily furious, but there was nothing I could do. I paused, sat down and reflected on my extra time in Philadelphia, and on the irony of the evening. I wondered what to do. I thought about the extra time in Philadelphia. Was I supposed to miss the flight? Were there people I was supposed to meet on my later flight, whom I would not have ordinarily met? Was I was supposed to use the extra time to write something significant or read something that would change my perspective and enrich my life? I did not know, but I was determined to look for the blessing as I waited for the next flight. I had a nice evening talking with the passengers on my new flight. The evening went fast. I arrived home safely, without an additional dose of tension. I made the most of the flight delay and experienced multiple blessings.

I remembered situations where I was late leaving the house on my way to work. One obstacle after another erupted to block my path. Invariably, on my way to work, I would see a driver who was involved in an accident or a car pulled over by a police officer to the side of the road, apparently for speeding. I wondered, if I had left home on time, would I have been in the accident or received the speeding ticket? I retrospectively began counting the situations as blessings; however, I wasn't thinking that way at the time.

When we face circumstances beyond our control; when we experience misfortune or hard times, rather than bemoaning our plight, placing blame or losing our composure, we should make the most of the time and look for the blessing. We should search for the jewel that is buried in the situation. We should look for the secrets, the lessons and treasures hidden in the moment. There is therapeutic value in having the right attitude and the proper perspective. After all, we control our perspectives, our attitudes and our responses to the circumstances we encounter. God has placed a gift for us, a very special blessing that is imbedded in each moment. It is up to us to learn from our experiences to add richness and adventure to our lives. We should look for the blessing as a prize given to us in each situation as a gift.

$\mathcal{A}$cknowledgements

The idea for this book came from numerous e-mails and verbal comments sent by people who read my first book *Teach the Children to Dance.* I was touched by the number of references to the inspirational feelings people experienced from the book. Several people mentioned keeping the book on their nightstand. The outpouring of support led me to write and compile another anthology of my emotions. This body of work centers on inspirational topics gleaned from my life and the lives of others who have shared their stories with me.

We have so many reasons to be thankful. Living in the greatest nation on the planet and surrounded by freedoms that many take for granted should make it easy for us to look for the blessings in our lives. However, this is easier said than done.

I owe my parents for my optimistic disposition. I grew up in a home where hope was present along with a daily message of our potential. My mother used to say I was the chosen one. She didn't tell me why I was chosen or what I was chosen to do. She said it was up to God to reveal Himself and it was up to me to find out what He wanted me to do.

In my parents' home, we were often told that everything would be alright if we just trusted in the Lord. We knew that the Lord would make a way somehow. This upbringing helped shape my faith and gave me the perspective I needed to complete any assignment.

I would like to thank everyone in the company I've worked for over the past twenty-seven years. We were the Stuart Company, Stuart Pharmaceuticals, ICI Pharma, Zeneca and now AstraZeneca. I was mentored and inspired by many competent caring individuals who stimulated my creativity and desire for excellence. They also held me accountable for high levels of ethical conduct, delivering results and being a role model.

My spiritual development and service-oriented mentality was cultivated at Antioch Baptist Church in Cleveland, Ohio. I was ordained a deacon by Reverend Dr. Marvin A. McMickle and the Deacon Board. The Deacons and the Sunday School Department teachers were major influences on my life.

My growth was further encouraged while serving on the Drama Team and Career Ministries at WillowCreek Community Church in South Barrington, Illinois. I cannot begin to explain the work that God has engineered in my life in this environment of God-centered people. Pastors Bill Hybels, John and Nancy Ortberg and Nancy Beach have motivated me to grow in many ways. Steve Pederson, Mark Demel, Rod and Deanna Armentrout have stretched me through the drama training. I am grateful to Curt Baer, Bill Muhr, Ruth Groth, Mike Patterson and the rest of the leaders in the Career's Ministry for including me in their work. The value of their contributions to help people find the work God designed for them is monumental.

I am indebted to my daughter, Veronica Ceaser for her willingness to contribute to my work by providing subject matter and reading the manuscript. Additionally, I thank Sue Vlahos, my administrative assistant for her critical eye in reviewing my work and adding her comments.

Alone with my thoughts

When I am alone with thoughts,
I am not lonely.
I do not feel abandoned;
I am not bored,
For God is my companion,
And in the company
Of infinite memories,
My Lord comforts me.

When I am alone with my thoughts,
I do not feel ignored,
For solitude refreshes
And satiates my spirit.
The still small voice is audible
And I hear it speaking softly,
As I climb down from lofty
Expectations.
I know that in God's eyes,
I don't need a disguise
To be accepted.

When I am alone with my thoughts,
I delve beneath the dermis of the stream.
I descend beyond shallow excursions
And risk the unthinkable and stretch my dreams
To adventures and exotic diversions
That require me to bend my mind,
To think hard and transcend my mind,

To seek, to contemplate, to find
My way to inner peace.

When I am alone with my thoughts,
God is there with me,
And if I sought His counsel,
I would be taught marvelous things.

America responds

America responds
In unity;
Differences are set aside
As the community
Rallies to comfort the afflicted
In their lamentation.

America responds
With compassion
And forces that divide
Us are deactivated,
And restricted,
As we unite our nation.

America responds,
With patriotic
Expressions of pride
In this great land,
And everything

For which it stands.
America responds
By rolling up her sleeves
And getting back to business,
To ensure that evil
Doesn't get the upper hand.
America opens her heart
And her store houses,
While she grieves,
For she understands
That mourning should
Not be brief,
That generosity
Should not be paralyzed
By her grief.

America responds
Within her character.
Her personality
Condemns terrorism
And shows contempt
For brutality.
When victimized,
No criminal is exempt
From her mighty hand;
For her call to justice
Is swift to reprimand.

America will stand

America will stand,
Despite the terror,
The acts of violence.
She will endure,
For calamity will unite us and
Stoke the flames of patriotism.
America will mourn and bury her children
But not in silence.
Although distraught,
And intermittently sobbing,
She screams
At the images of sorrow.
America has taught
Us to be strong,
When evil is intent on robbing
Us of freedom;
To be triumphant over wrong
So tomorrow,
Righteousness will still prevail;
And justice will be consistent;
For justice will not fail.

America will stand
For freedom and justice
And will not compromise
The values upon which
This country was founded.
America, will defy evil and rise

In spirit for she is grounded
In principles universal and just.
She is near to God
And in God the trust
Grows stronger.

America will stand,
Although the landscape changed,
She is majestic in her grief;
Although she is estranged
From some of her people,
The separation will be brief.
America will stand,
Weeping, angered by the violation,
As she cares for her people
On the eve of retaliation.

Another day above ground

The Lord has spoken,
The wounded shall be healed
And the lost shall be found.
His body was broken
As He rose to reveal
Another day above ground.

We should be mindful
That love infiltrates and heals
In a manner that's profound.

Instead of pushing up daisies
He continues to amaze me,
With another day above ground.

To spend time complaining,
About the insignificant
Is ludicrous as it sounds.
So take the time remaining,
Which is magnificent,
As another day above ground.

He grants us consciousness,
As portals to creation
So that we may abound
In beauty, as we coalesce
To show appreciation
For another day above ground.

Another day without His love

You're active daily in the race
As you succumb to life's demands.
You look in mirrors seeking grace
And search for fairness in the land.
The battle lines upon your face
Confess your will to understand.

In public you proclaim self made,
Religion's for the weak not strong.

You pass it off as some charade
To be trivialized in song.
In private quarters you're afraid,
For senses tell you something's wrong.

And it is just
Another day without His love;
Another day you doubt His love
And God seems just
Someone you must
Dismiss.
Another day where you maintain,
There is no God to ease your pain,
And life is naught but loss and gain,
Where you implore,
There must be more
Than this!

You're cynical and out of bounds.
The world dictates how you behave.
You say through research you have found,
There is not life beyond the grave.
But deep inside you hear the sounds
Of spirits wailing to be saved.

You say pretense is wasting time,
Revoke the primitive and live!
But emptiness besets your climb,
You're running as a fugitive
Who knows that he has met the crime
But won't ask Jesus, Judge forgive.

And it is just,
Another day without His love;
Another day you doubt His love.
A waste of time;
A paradigm,
Absurd.
Another day that arguments,
Rise to defeat you and prevents
The joy that Jesus represents.
The fount of peace,
Accounts for peace.
And you exist
And don't resist,
His word.

Until then it's just
Another day without His love;
Another day you doubt His love
And God seems just
Someone you must
Dismiss.
Another day where you maintain,
There is no God to ease your pain
And life is naught but loss and gain,
Where you implore,
There must be more
Than this!

Because His love

His love lives in controversy.
It asks you to come for mercy.
Before emergencies,
Seek Him urgently,
Because His love,
Was created for you.

His love may evoke suspicion;
But He is the Great Physician.
His love heals and restores
And His goodness is yours,
Because His love,
Was created for you.

His stamina is stupendous;
Consistency is tremendous;
A love outrageous
And advantageous,
Because His love
Was created for you.

The tenderness of sacrifice;
The promises of paradise;
His love is specific,
In touch and terrific,
Because His love,
Was created for you.

Blessed beyond belief

As you survey the patterns of your life,
Love interwoven, forms a motif
That strengthened the fabric of your life
And says you are the chosen one,
And blessed beyond belief.

Life is synonymous with light,
The spectrum and the components
Are filtered through a prism of time;
The joyous days adjacent to sad moments;
The ridiculous parallels the sublime
And time together rivals time alone.
Emotions range from gratitude to grief,
The positive persist with the negative bands
And sticks and stones may break your bones,
But you are blessed beyond belief.

When sorrow visits, the seeds are planted
To lower you into a grave of remorse,
So memory says don't take for granted
The special moments which are a source
Of pleasure.
Ensure that all debts are paid,
Which includes compliments,
Because your time is brief.
Be free of guilt, repent and know God prayed,
And gave you a blessing beyond belief.

When you think of all the circumstances
And all the places you could have landed.
When you think of all the many chances,
Of the times you escaped when stranded,
You should be thankful for the choices,
For moments of exertion and relief.
Life has its faults, but your soul rejoices,
For you are blessed beyond belief.

Delight in your gray hairs

Delight in your gray hairs;
Majestic are they, as silken filaments
That highlight your face.
They show your involvement;
That you didn't merely take up space.
You absorbed the scenery
When you went around the block.
Your eyes were not closed
Or spent watching the clock.

Delight in your gray hairs;
They communicate and acknowledge
That you have lived
And spent time climbing stairs,
And shared in what took place.
You didn't simply run in place,
You extended yourself,
And though you didn't medal or place,
You were consistently in the race.

Delight in your gray hairs;
The silver strands of experience,
The frosted slivers of wise perspectives,
Gained by not asking for clearance
To initiate every action;
Evidence that you became selective,
As you learned about cause and effect,
That every action,
Had an equal and opposite reaction;
That objects in motion or at rest
Remained that way unless
An intervention from an outside
Or internal force,
Changed its nature
Or altered their course.

Delight in your gray hairs,
The ribbons you've earned
In life's struggles,
Which taught you the merit
Of managing your affairs;
That taught you to juggle
Multiple agenda items, skillfully;
To be a quick study
Even an unwilling student,
As you received,
On the battlefield training.

Delight in your gray hairs;
They are your medals of honor,
For meritorious service,

For valor beyond the call of duty.
Wear them with honor
For they can symbolize
The glory, the beauty,
The wisdom of a life
Well lived and lived
To its fullest in God.

Do not abandon me

Do not abandon me
For I am aging.
I savor life,
Reading each line
For maximum effect.
I was not paging
Through the manuscript.
I memorized my part
And spoke love to you
From a trusting heart.

Do not abandon me
As irrelevant fiction,
Filled with formulas,
Whose predictions
Have no significance.
I was there as we read
To each other,
As we broke bread

With each other
In the name of romance.

Be sensitive to history
For my eyes document
The shared sunsets,
Embraces that arched
Over heart beats
To connect our memories.
Do not abandon me because
My eyes witnessed
When your lips moved
And swore to never leave me
And taught me what love meant
And blessed the covenant
We made to each other
As we reinvented ourselves
And presented ourselves
As an eternal union.

I sit on a mountaintop
But I am not over the hill.
I am pensive, contemplating
The crest of my life,
While reflecting on
The rest of my life,
Knowing full well that
The best of my life
Is framed as a couple.

Do not abandon me
When I change my gait,
Reduce my speed and acquire
A fear of being on my own,
As I learn to adjust and compensate,
Requiring assistance
To do the things
That I once did alone.

Remember the golden age
Of our relationship;
Recall our renaissance,
When we revived
The vows of love;
When we rekindled the priceless
Pleasures of partnering;
And aimed for longevity
In our commitment.

I am what I think of myself;
What I choose to be.
I am not ancient,
But I have antique qualities.
I am a landmark,
Not a dilapidated dwelling.
My heart is bi-spiritual,
Bilateral and bilingual.
I feel, exist and speak in pairs
But I am one in relationship.

Do not abandon me
For I am aging.
I savor life,
I am in this with you,
Reading each line
For maximum effect,
Not merely paging
Through the manuscript.
Do not abandon me.
I shared genesis with you.
I was there when we had
Nothing;
Only a dream, a passion,
An obsession,
That gave us an identity.

aith

Have faith in the power of your influence
In the early years.
Be confident.
The amnesia of your children will not last.
The anesthesia will pass,
And they will sense your pain
And shed tears of repentance.

Have faith in the power of your influence
In the early years.
The values stored in the misguided vessels,

Will be discovered and will be used to steer
Them back to an honorable course;
For guilt will cause them to wrestle
With the agony of remorse.

Have faith in the power of your influence
In the early years.
Know that one day,
Your progeny will step clear of the ether.
Their lungs will gasp to
Inhale the air of redemption.
They will face you, embrace you,
And do the unthinkable.
They will plead for exemption
From the wages of disobedience,
And in earnest,
Ask for love
And beg for your forgiveness.

Faith, family and occupation

Faith, family and occupation
A proper ranking is the goal.
For blessings flourish in relation
To the extent of God's control
In our lives.

When He is first
He governs every week

And schedules reflect His leanings.
He's manifested
In the words we speak.
He grants our lives
A richer meaning.

If we disrupt
The sanctioned series,
Change the sequence
For the pride of man,
The substitute would yield
Failed theories,
That would contradict
The Savior's Plan.

A life designed
In perfect order,
Has God as primary,
Lord above.
He penetrates more
Than the borders.
He is ubiquitous
With His love.

Faith, family and occupation
The proper ranking is the goal.
For blessings flourish in relation
To the extent of God's control
In our lives.

amily

We have to play together better
And learn each other's blind spots,
Our strengths and weaknesses.
We need to demonstrate a cooperative spirit
To pitch in and pick each other up after a fall.
When one of us is in a slump,
All must go to the member with the hot hand
And cheer the one who is lagging behind.

We must understand
That we must band together
And double team the oppressor
And form a fence around our kin.
We must help free those in bondage,
And release the strength within
Our lineage.

We are a family
That must sacrifice for the good
Of our kindred.
These truths should be common knowledge;
As instinctive as genetic information.
These rules should be understood
And taught, to give pride to our nation.
They should be woven into daily living,
In joyous love filled celebration.

Fight for your people

I must fight for your people.
I must boldly stand my ground,
Until their eyes are opened
And the lost among them found.

I must fight for your people,
By your grace the debt has been paid;
Souls have been redeemed and made
Free, no longer prisoners bound
By sin as your spirit surrounds
Them with love as their shield;
To comfort them on the battlefield.

I must fight for your people,
With every breath and waking prayer;
Remove the scales from their eyes
To show them your vision for their lives
And to the enemy, boldly declare
That I am my Father's disciple,
And as long as I have breath
I swear to be there,

To fight for your people
And speak to them, attend and enforce
The teachings of the master strategist;
So they will prosper and gain wisdom
From the omnipotent source
Of every good and perfect gift.

For Your word will empower and lift
Their faith as the wind to the dorsal wing.

I must fight for your people,
For I was commissioned to bring
Them to the Good Shepherd,
To their God Almighty, and
Righteous King.

Grounded

When your life is synchronized
And you are on a roll,
Don't settle into a comfort zone.
Your life is whirling,
Swirling under control,
Remember you are not alone.
No matter who's watching,
Walk the talk
And the roots are as important
As the more visible stalk.

So be grounded,
Always help others,
Don't forget their names
Or stare through them
Like they don't exist.
Reach out to them

Treat everyone the same
And lift them up
As others have lifted you.

And always strive to be wise.
Don't be confounded;
Face the world with opened eyes,
Seek to be grounded
In all you say and do
For God is expecting
This much from you.

He gave you life

He gave you life
And more abundantly.
He made you unique,
Not a redundancy.

He formed your will
And your tenacity.
You are essential,
Not excess capacity.

For your maturity
He gave you His gift.
It's called security
On the eternal shift.

He gave you life
And more abundantly.
He made you unique,
Not a redundancy.

*H*e has gifted us

He has gifted us
As instruments vibrating
So His joy flows through us,
Expressing the richness of His love.
He has lifted us
As His word is titrating
And breaking us down to rise above
Individual agendas that might
Confuse believers and block His light.

He has gifted us.
Each personal story contains
A song of God, transforming hearts.
He has shifted us
Into the light to give Him glory.
When people view the performing arts,
We are the vehicles, the vessels, the voices
That focus on the Savior and rejoices.

We are blessed with a heavenly mission
To rain God's love, so the droplets
Fall so they can strategically land

Where they can salvage the sinful condition.
He made the artists and the prophets
To help those in darkness to understand.

We may have drifted
From His word;
But each day He sifted
Through the world to find us.
He has gifted us
To undergird
And deliver a message
That reminds us
We are to be strong
And proclaim
And bless His Holy Name
In all the earth.

*H*e is the way

I cannot provide the help you need,
But through my faith I recommend
That you consult the Father.
For you need more than a friend,
You need someone to comfort and attend
To the deeper issues;
Someone who made you;
Someone who knows the mechanics
Of your being;
Someone all knowing;
Someone all seeing;

My help is insufficient,
For I am too limited in my scope.
I know not the words to say.
But I can point to the Father,
For He is your hope,
For He is the way.

$\mathcal{H}$e scaled the fortress

He scaled the fortress I created
To keep deities at bay.
I sorted techniques antiquated,
As I fought to keep Him away.

But He used methods and manners
Elaborate as needed for me;
A pillar of clouds in the day;
A pillar of fire at night;
As He stood in the river of my sin.

I picked up the blood-stained banner.
The waters receded for me.
He was the herald to guide my way
And if I keep Him in my sight,
He will work wonders from within.

He scaled the fortress I created
To keep deities at bay,
But I underestimated

The strength of His love,
The power of His sway.

$\mathcal{H}$e wants me to go on

If I take a step,
He will walk with me
And through His pep talk
I'm able to see
He wants me to go on.
If I take a stand,
He's touching my hand.
His energy
Flows near to me
And says,
To be strong,
For He wants me to go on.

When I am sitting
In despair
With thoughts of quitting
In the air,
He wants me to go on.
And when I breathe
I believe,
He wants me to go on.

Hero worship

I want a hero
Not an illusion.
I want consistency
Amidst the confusion.

I want a model
Where I can trace the design.
I want to emulate
An icon that's divine.

Holy Father, full of grace,
Take me to a holy place.
Let me see Jesus
Consistently,
When I hero worship,
Let it be You that I see.

Adoration
Can be misplaced,
In a mortal man
Who can be disgraced.

I need a standard
That's beyond reproach.
I need The Comforter
To serve as my coach.

We are inspired by His Holy Word
To be lifted higher by the One preferred.
No idol worship will suffice for me,
When I hero worship,
Let it be You that I see.

$\mathscr{H}$e is there

Daily,
He does not fail me.
Nightly,
He is right for me.
Weekly,
He speaks to me.
Each day He finds a way
To share that He is there.

Daily,
When evil assails me
He is connected
To me in prayer.
Hourly,
He empowers me.
Each minute
He is in it
To care
For He is there.

Hey Lord! Look at me!

You have,
Provided for me.
You have divided the sea
So I could feel safety inside.
Dear Lord,
You have confided in me
And I decided to be
A person you look to with pride.

Hey Lord! Look at me!
My mind is on obeying
Your teachings.
The worship and the praying
Is reaching
And challenging me to do more.
Hey Lord! Look at me!
I'm working on forgiving
And trying
To learn from your living
And dying
That I should give thanks to you more.

For your sweet attention
I hurry to mention
How much I have done.
In my works and in my heart
I know you set me apart
To serve you as the only one.

I want You to be proud
For your love has allowed
Me to grow and give You glory.
Generous in latitude
You have shaped my attitude
Into a compelling story.

Hey Lord! Look at me!
I'm working on forgetting
Indignities and letting
Your grace penetrate my soul.
Hey Lord! Look at me!
Restoring the family
Exploring who I am to be
To impress you
As I live my role.

Hey Lord! Look at me!
My mind is on obeying
Your teachings.
The worship and the praying
Is reaching
And challenging me to do more.
Hey Lord! Look at me!
I'm working on forgiving
And trying
To learn from your living
And dying
That I should give thanks to you more.

His love is infinite

Some set out to build corporations
And others to establish nations.
He set out to give salvation
Without a fee.

Some set out to build an empire;
Some a career to take them higher.
He builds lives and nurtures a fire
That burns in me.

He builds a family from the core
And enters my life through the open door.
He gives us life that we can live it more
Abundantly.

Some set out to search for promise lands;
Some reputations behind which they stand.
His love is infinite and it expands
Eternity.

How great is love?

How great is love, if with its might
A coward can be made to fight;
A miser made to lose his greed
And share with those who are in need?

How great is love, if with its grace
It can forgive a man disgraced
And sympathize with those of us
Who have lost someone close to us?

How great is love, if with its care
It can uplift one from despair;
And comfort those in times of grief
Whose souls play beggar to relief?

How great is love, if with its song
It can inspire a man along
And render forth the strength that may
Propel him through another day?

How great is love, if with its charms
It can entreat me to your arms
And there entice me with its art
Until it confiscates my heart?

How great is love, if with its might
A coward can be made to fight;
A miser made to lose his greed
And share with those who are in need?

$\mathcal{I}$ could serve you better

I crave competition.
I should remove
My stubborn adherence
To something to prove;
I know that my neighbor
Is equal to me.
I could serve You better
If I would let this be.

If I discarded
All my disloyal friends,
I won't be bombarded
When I want to spend
More of my time serving,
And giving my all.
I could serve You better
If I answered Your call.

I've seen advertising,
That's seductive to me.
I am criticizing
The fallen society.
I'm made superior,
If I risk a chance.
I could serve You better
Or by some circumstance.

If I could get out of the way
And trust You, love and obey,
Uphold the covenant
And follow through.
I could serve You better
If I became more like you.

Worship You daily
Study Your word
Though men may fail me
I remember I heard
The voice on the mountain
Through Moses ears.
I could serve You better
If I acknowledge You're here.

*I*n God's Time

In God's Time,
The people will be there,
As answered prayer,
To lift you
From the depths of despair.
In God's Time,
The materials you need
To assemble the task,
Along with the instructions,
Will be present,
Sometimes while you pray
And sometimes before you ask.

In God's Time,
You won't be shunned.
You will have the resources.
You will have the funds.
The cupboards will be stocked
And your debts paid.
The enemy in shock
Will turn and run afraid.

In God's Time,
The unruly child will bless your name.
The unruly spirit will succumb, tamed
As the open hand defies the fist;
The gentle spirit will insist
That vengeance for each crime,
Be cast aside.
In God's Time
We will face the amnesia
Of a saved heart,
When God gives justice
At His anointed time.

In God's Time,
We will no longer
Be abused.
The intimidators, perpetrators
Of unrighteousness will be excused;
Confessed sins will be forgiven and
Removed from inventory,
And with a clean slate
We will dance in Glory;
In God's Time.

I do not live in the past

I do not live in the past,
But I visit it often,
Through the music of my youth;
Through memories
That have no copyright protection;
Through phrases that have been passed down
To the current generation;
Through images on television
And the trains of thought
That are an invitation to time travel.

I do not live in the past,
But I visit it often,
In conversations on how things were;
Through the revisionist musings
Of nostalgic mental promenades,
Through the archives of my life.
I search for answers to present
Day scenarios.
I search for patterns and trends
That would enable me to support or defend
A stance I am contemplating.
I stand with a hand full of puzzle pieces,
Wondering where to place them.
I search for my ancestors
With the nerve to face them,
To explain what I've done with my life.

I do not live in the past,
But I visit it often,
To hear kind words spoken to me
When I accomplished little things;
For encouragement and nourishment,
For compliments and smiles
That levitated my spirit
Before my consecutive string
Of happy times was broken.

I sit in the old familiar chairs;
Pose again for the photographs
That are now in the picture albums;
Create deja vu moments
From the basic ingredients.
I hold the ones I love.

I tell them I love them.
I speak the promises
Which I will remember,
While sampling friendships
As fine chocolates
Or homemade bread.

I live in the present.
I travel in the current day,
The current moment
And the current year of our Lord;
But occasionally, I take long walks
As I visit my old stomping grounds,
The familiar surroundings.

I sort through issues
That are rooted in my past.
I experience the joy, peace, forgiveness
And pain from previous encounters.
I sift enthusiastically through the chest
Of childhood and adult memorabilia.
But, I always face the reality
That I could never stay there,
For I am a resident of the present.

I do not live in the past,
But, I visit it often.
It brings me pleasure and perspective;
To see the environments and remind myself
That I am blessed and should be thankful
To be a recipient of God's loving and saving grace.

I picture God

I picture God with a wheelbarrow
As He carts away my sins;
While standing in the straight and narrow,
Directing traffic from within.

His eye is on the sparrow
As He clothes the lilies of the field.
He demonstrated to Pharaoh
That He's my armor and my shield.

I can see God shaking His head.
His patience should be wearing thin.
The things I've done, the words I've said
Define the trouble that I'm in.

I am so thankful that He cares
For sinful soldiers who repent,
Who travel lonely thoroughfares
To save the lost and discontent.

I picture God with a wheelbarrow
As He carts away my sins;
He consecrates the straight and narrow
And plants the Holy One within,
To teach us that we might follow;
To fill us when we are hollow;
So that we comprehend the loss
Of His sacrifice on the cross.

I prayed for you today

I prayed for you today;
That problems that come your way,
Would dissipate into the air,
And look as though, they've not been there,
As God helps you to understand.

I prayed for you this morning,
That you may have a warning,

To give you a chance to prepare,
To brace yourself, so you can bear
The tribulations of this land.

I prayed for you this evening;
That illness would be leaving
A stronger person in your bed,
With vital strength to go ahead,
To tell who made you whole.

I prayed for you tonight;
Relationships are right,
For people in conflict to compromise
And realize that hurt filled lies
Are a poison to the soul.

I prayed for you today;
That problems that come your way,
Would dissipate into the air
And God would follow you
Everywhere.

I rose to love

I did not fall in love;
I rose to love.
I heard the call of love
And chose to love.
My eyes were open
I knew where I was.
Love lifted me,
That's what it does.

I did not tumble,
Fall head over heels.
My heart was humble,
For I felt love was real.
I was not cavalier
To strike a pose for love.
For honest and sincere,
Is how one goes to love.

Without a thunder clap
Or being taken by surprise;
Not under a spell to snap
Out of and awaken my eyes.
I used my head to analyze
What touched my heart,
When love said to rise.

I did not fall in love;
I rose to love.

I heard the call to love
So I was exposed to love.
I was not apprehended.
I was not suspended.
But I chose to love,
And I ascended.

I worship you

I worship You outdoors
For the earth is yours
And the fullness thereof;
While walking near the sea
I find myself visually
Responding to your love.

I worship You indoors,
In offices, in stores,
From an escalators view;
While sitting in my chair
Admitting time spent there,
Is giving thanks to You.

I worship you in solitude,
On liquid snacks and solid food,
In personal exploration;
While nourishing my attitude
Or serving to show gratitude,
I pause in adoration.

I worship You rising
And when exercising,
When working and on break.
Before my work is done,
I focus on your Son,
In His name and for His sake.

I worship You in my routine.
I schedule private time to glean
Moments to marvel on Your ways;
On the train and in the car,
My relationship so far
Wants to give glory and to praise.

I take moments to marvel on Your ways;
To read your story and give praise;
To give You glory and to praise.

It will take Jesus to repair my soul

Hearts broken as a sign of my youth;
Unkind words spoken, that veered from the truth;
Accumulated a lifetime of hurt,
It quenched my hunger to roll in the dirt.

It would take many lifetimes to forgive;
To work off damage from the way I lived,
But finally it has taken its toll,
It will take Jesus to repair my soul.

On rare occasions I've had evil thoughts;
Acts of evasion that were never caught;
At times my actions were out of control.
It will take Jesus to repair my soul.

My sinful nature must be held to blame.
I need a pardon to conceal my shame.
His broader shoulders on a loving frame,
I need the refuge of his Holy Name

The skeletons are in my secret place;
Fear of discovery is on my face.
I feel the emptiness, I feel a hole.
It will take Jesus to repair my soul.

*J*esus and mother

The Holy Scriptures void of myth
Were taught to me while in the fifth
Year at the church, New Morning Star.
I was inquisitive, but shy
With burning questions to clarify;
Why God is near, yet seems so far?
Why evil is allowed to roam?
Why Satan calls this planet home?

These questions greeted the arrival
Of the church's annual revival;
The greatest show on God's green earth.
The mourner's bench was center stage,

And there the sinner's would engage
The Holy Spirit to rebirth,
Until Jesus our Lord and Savior
Brought about a new behavior.

It was within this element
Of Father, Son and devilment,
That I sought refuge in my youth.
I needed serenity
As I searched for identity;
Though fearful I would find the truth,
Which would destroy my self-esteem
And cast doubt's shadow on my dreams.

I found myself thus predisposed
To Jesus, fish and barely loaves,
As a child to his mother's breast.
He came to earth that I might live,
Forgets repented wrongs, forgives
The several secret sins confessed.
Through his eternal love alone,
I sensed maternal undertones.

Through miracles his love expressed
As manifested tenderness;
A calm word to a troubled sea.
His strength, unselfish sacrifice
Invited me to paradise,
To his bosom to comfort me.
As we drifted to each other,
Jesus seemed a lot like mother.

$\mathscr{L}$ook for the blessing

In life's adventures and catastrophes,
When bad things happened magnetically,
I spent considerable energy
In anger, unhappy, impatiently
Driven, then it occurred to me
That it could help me
Become stress free,
If I looked for the blessing.

When leaving my house late
And the traffic was delayed,
Once frustrated, I never displayed
A sense of reverence,
I never prayed
Or took the time,
To look for the blessing.

I've learned there is a purpose in events.
I may have been spared pain and accidents
Or met new challenges that God presents
When He wants me to look for the blessing.

Things happen for His reason
According to God's plan.
We are too busy to seize them
And take the time to scan
Our surroundings to handle
What we can

Or in essence,
To look for the blessing.

Lord what must I do in this pain?
You want more of me than to complain.
I know in the circumstances
A blessing is contained,
And I should look for the blessing.

There have been setbacks
But I have found,
That if I take the focus off of me
And look around,
There's a message in a bottle,
Directions to higher ground
If I look for the blessing.

I should seek the opportunity to grow
To render kindness or to bestow
A gift to a stranger,
Or meet someone I need to know
As I look for the blessing.

$\mathcal{L}$ord, how strong do you think I am?

Lord, how strong do you think I am?
I find myself on the brink of disaster.
But since I am linked to you,
I feel I can master anything.
Each day brings new dilemmas and trials,
My spirit bends but does not break,
I try to face suffering with smiles,
But you know my tolerance level
And how much I can take.

Lord, I am sinking in my sorrow
I find hope thinking of your love.
Your comfort allows me to borrow
The strength I need to match my strain.
In your eyes, I must be Gibraltar,
For when I am weak and starting to falter,
I'm given access to your grace
And your threshold for pain.

Lord, when my shoulders are drooping
And I stand imperfectly, stooping
Under the weight of my cares.
When my balance is challenged,
And nerves are shaking,
I wonder if you are mistaking
Me for someone with a greater capacity
To withstand the wear and tear
Of this life;

For you said you wouldn't give me
More than I could bear.

Lord, how strong do you think I am?
I find myself on the brink of disaster.
But since I am linked to you,
I feel I can master anything.
Each day brings new dilemmas and trials,
My spirit bends but does not break,
I try to face suffering with smiles,
For you know my tolerance level
And how much I can take.

$\mathscr{L}$ord, I marvel

Lord, I marvel at the magnitude of your restraint.
Your anger should overflow and cause you to faint
From my rebellious ways.
When I am insolent and disobedient,
You could shorten my days,
But your mercy is expedient.

Lord, I marvel at the magnitude of your restraint.
You give me latitude that should be reserved for a saint.
You allow me to benefit from your grace.
Within your tender heart,
Your love is training me,
Modeling patience
And sustaining me.

Lord, lead me to wisdom

Lord lead me to wisdom
And spare me of your wrath;
Improve my decisions
Place me on the righteous path.

Lord lead me to wisdom
To the higher and holy ground
Away from my own devises;
Where your mercy can be found.
Lord lead me to wisdom
Patience when your advice is
To stay the course, when sacrifice is
Your answer in a crisis,
For Christ is,
For Christ is.

Lord, what are your intentions?

Lord,
What are your intentions
With me?
Now that we are alone
What will it be?
Now that I am yours,
I'm anxious to see,
What your intentions are with me?

I spent life spurning religions.
I searched for the perfect fit,
But their words and their decisions
Left me unable to commit.
But rumors flew and people said
Peculiar stories with advice
About you rising from the dead,
After the perfect sacrifice.

Lord,
What are your intentions
With me?
Now that we are alone
What will it be?
Now that I am yours,
I'm anxious to see,
What your intentions are with me?

My question is rhetorical
And broad in its scope.
Your wisdom is historical;
Your word is my hope.
My faith is not empty;
Your promises aren't deferred,
Though Satan may tempt me,
There is protection in your word.

The evidence is clear.
The proof has clarity.
And now that I'm yours,

It's easy to see,
What your intentions are with me.

I have the blessed assurance;
The peace that passes understanding.
You gave me the endurance
For when life is demanding
So that I might see,
What your intentions are with me.

$\mathcal{L}$ord, who am I that you should notice me?

Lord,
Who am I that you should notice me?
I have not fame that would impress
A holy wise God, who's name
Is imprinted on every gene.
Who am I that the Master would address
His humble servant with love
Though I consciously rebel
And fail to worship you consistently?

Who am I that you should notice me?
At this stage of my development,
Lacking maturity, possessing talents
And elements that are not relevant
To attract your attention.
I daily wrestle with ingrown flaws

And acquire new ones
With the circadian rhythms of the heart.

My soul is blemished.
Spiritual acne covers the epidermis
Of my heart and I am ashamed.
I try to disguise my ailment, my motives,
But they are disclosed to you,
For you are all knowing.

I am predisposed to selfish acts.
I can't suppose that you react
Admiringly to my insignificance.
I'm prone to compare myself to others
And others to me.
I judge and sentence the innocent
As if my decree
Has value or merit.
I try to deny that I did inherit
Traits of imperfections.
I am frequently lost
But I give directions
To others upon the road.
I've seen my brother struggle
And not offered to share
Or lighten his load.

Lord,
Who am I that you should notice me?
I am a grain of sand upon the ocean floor;
Yet your actions state that you adore me.

In an over populated world,
I am a speck upon the solar system;
Yet your eyes pierce through the crowds
And galaxies,
Through layers of nonsense and deception,
Through artificial images and intelligence
To speak to me as if I am the only one.
What have I said?
What have I done?
Why should you take the time
And make the effort to notice me,
To send me your Son?

What is it about me?
Or am I being presumptuous
And self-centered?
What is it about you
That would finance a rescue mission
To lift me from my plight
In my condition.
Why journey across a universe
To one such as I, drenched in sin.
One who improves, relapses,
Makes progress then gets worse;
One who is incomplete, in denial,
Who stands on the precipice of defeat?
I am perennially on parole,
Awaiting trial for multiple offenses.
As a repeat offender
I fall short of your expectations,
But there is something about you;

There is love about you as you send tender
Messages of encouragement.
It is through your infinite love
That you manifest patience.

I should be insignificant in a world vast
And incomprehensible,
But you took the time and through
A sensible act of kindness,
Placed mud on the eyes of my soul
And lifted the blindness
And told me I was important,
Because I was important to you.
And now I, your humble creation
Will act in faith and obligation,
To exercise the options, the free will,
The choice,
To accept you and voice
My testimonial to the ends of the earth.

$\mathcal{L}$ove is a battered soldier

Love is a battered soldier;
Worn and ragged from years of wear,
Withstanding the corrosive elements of time,
During the long and eventful journey across deserts
Dangerous jungles on the road to paradise;
Enduring the onslaught of warring factions,

The excursions across enemy lines,
And the strengthening and debilitating challenges of time
And temptations.

Love is a tattered soldier,
It's uniform losing the starched, pressed appearance of newness.
However the buckles and buttons shine through the encounters.
And when the battle is over and the victory is secured,
The uniform will be refurbished;
The torn and worn fabric repaired,
As we marvel at the decorated soldier
With stronger fibers and brilliant colors.

$\mathcal{L}$ove walks the avenues

Love walks the avenues,
The boulevards and drives
And parkways and circles.
Love is active.
Love is alive.
Love walks the roads and highways,
Silent lanes and crowded streets,
Where the pedestrians
Play and compete.
Love is on the move.
Love has something to prove.

Love rides in taxicabs
And chauffeured limousines.
As back seat drivers

In the family machines.
Sedans, convertibles
And minivans,
Depict its presence
According to plan.
Love knows the system;
You can't resist him.
Love hears the whispers,
You can't resist her.
Love is on the move.
Love has something to prove.

Love sits in cable cars and submarines;
While on trains, we sip caffeine;
The same on cruise ships and other boats,
Some motored powered
Vehicles that float.
Love and all its variations
Are with us on all forms
Of transportation.
Love travels in many ways
It's all around you.
It plays and stays.
Love is on the move.
Love has something to prove.

Love walks the avenues
The boulevards and drives,
The parkways and circles
Love is active.
Love is alive.

Love is on the roads and highways,
Silent lanes and crowded streets.
Where pedestrians
Play and compete.
Love is on the move.
Love has something to prove.

an

I am an appendage
Of the human race,
Attached at the soul;
A Siamese existence.
I stand a peninsula,
Not an island,
Sharing a coastline
With everyone;
A part of the mainland.

Treat me as family
In your relationship with me.
We are parent or progeny,
Blood of the same stream of Adam.
We are compatible,
For there is only one race
With many mountain ranges
Merging, intersecting
And overlapping.

Man segments and classifies.
We were given the command in Eden;
Name the animals one by one.
We are God's creations
From volcanic ash,
Molded by His hands
With the waters of eternal patience.

We spend our lives
Trying to emulate our maker,
But realize later in life
That we assemble and
Discover more than we create,
But when we create
The beauty brings us closer
To God.

ercy

Although armed with the reality that the inevitable
Will come sooner than expected;
You are still a hold out,
Doubting the evidence of the expiration date,
Banking on a miracle;
Hoping the Creator has a change of mind
And allows you a few more special moments;
A reprieve, an extension, a hung jury.

There you are standing before the Almighty;
Humbled by His significance,
Begging Him for more time;
Beseeching His benevolence,
Asking for compassion;
Asking that your wish be granted,
Not knowing that over the course of your life
He has already granted you
Many such wishes;
Without a request
And without your knowledge.

y joy

When at times I feel depressed
Over burdened and under stress.
I fail to realize how I am blessed
And it takes my joy away.

There are times when I compare
Myself to others and then I swear
That my life is empty, though God is there
And it takes my joy away.

When at times I am feeling low
Distracted from the overflow
Of problems that seem to plateau
And it takes my joy away

I must be centered on His grace;
For He entered the human race;
Died for my sins, He took my place,
So my joy would not go away.

My life

I need someone to help me grow,
To comprehend me;
To complement me,
Not with expectations
Of making me complete.

I need someone to help me grow,
Someone whom I know
Will be there as my soul mate.
Someone cognizant of my faults
And when I struggle with my fate,
To be actively involved
And sensitive in their suggestions
For improvement.

I need someone to enhance me,
To round off rough edges,
Not with pledges of a passive make-over.
I don't want a conqueror,
A competitor to takeover,
For it is still my life,
And I will be held accountable.

My prayer

God, thank you for this ability.
May I use it with humility;
Treat people with civility;
Display wisdom and stability.

May I have the visibility
So others will see your will in me.
Grant me strength against hostility
To show your love.

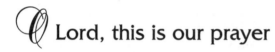

O Lord, this is our prayer

In our search for answers,
May we have clarity;
To approach those in need
With charity;
In our struggle against evil,
Solidarity;
This O Lord is our prayer.

On Valentine's Day

I wish you
A relationship that satisfies
And is fulfilling;
A need identified,
A companion who's willing
To place themselves second
And you first.

I wish you
A fairy-tale beginning
And happy ever after
The differences of the souls
Are rectified and winning
Is not as important
As the laughter
Which adds to the youthful appearance
Of your relationship.
I wish you
A bond based in reality,
To fortify it for the challenging ways
In which life installs hurdles.
I wish you love that is evolving
Into sweeter days
With surprises at every turn,
That is not creating more problems
Than it is solving,
That makes mistakes and learns
From them to minimize
Their presence at sunrise.

I wish your regrets be as storm clouds
That dissipate into minor concerns;
A spirit that anticipates
And yearns to live up to love's
Expectations,
Not those in the audience,
Not the people along the way.
I wish you love in all its splendor,
Bliss as you surrender
Amidst the promises to stay.
I wish you love on Valentine's Day.

People are more important than things

People are more important than things;
Relationships than objects possessed.
From the right correlation springs
Ingredients of true happiness.

People are more important than things;
Emotions than property we own;
For family and fulfillment clings
To the heart so we aren't alone.

Materials assets are prized.
We worship our status and wealth,
But the things that we have idolized,
Are worthless when losing our health.

Heirlooms and antiques can be scratched
And museum pieces restored;
Though sentimental value's attached,
They can't match the greatest reward.

People are more important than things;
More fragile than we would expect.
Consider the joy that it brings,
So don't let them suffer neglect.

Pray for our leaders

Pray for our leaders
Courageous, whether the battlefield
Is business, civics or religious;
Instructing us when to fight
And when to yield,
And whether the venue
Is ordinary or prestigious.
There, shoulder to shoulder
They're visionary
Decisions vary
With the situation.

Pray for our leaders
Those who are appointed,
Those who are anointed
By the touch of the Master's hand.
May they maintain composure

From the constant exposure
To different circumstances
Under their command.

ray without ceasing

Please pray without ceasing,
For God is releasing
His power, to make a great work in you.
A pause in your praying,
Just might be delaying
The hour to break,
For His rendezvous.

Please pray without ceasing,
For God is increasing
His work, all He needs, is an open door.
Just humble your spirit,
I'm sure He will hear it,
And move you as the breakers,
Shape the shore.

Please pray without ceasing,
For Jesus is teaching
Us to be humble and trust in His word.
When standing or kneeling,
We must keep appealing,
Until our prayers,
Are delivered and heard.
We send collective prayers,

While changing intensities.
We beseech His mercy,
Launching them from our knees.
The doorway to heaven
Receives each submission;
Absorbing petitions,
And the persistent pleas.

Please pray without ceasing,
For God is releasing
His power, to make a great work in you.
Don't pause in your praying,
You might be delaying,
The hour to break,
For His rendezvous.

Pretend it's the end

Pretend it's the end.
The doctors delivered the news,
An estimated time of departure is set;
Second opinions are exhausted.
The physicians are unanimous in their views.
Now it's up to you to make the finish memorable.
You can't be tentative, for you must not forget
Your willingness to comprehend
Your struggles, even near your untimely demise.

Pretend it's the end.
You have limited hours to spend

And window shopping and negotiating for the best price
For your time is worthless.
The value of each minute escalates exponentially.
You can't wait for good deeds to go on sale,
You must do them
And ask them to be done to you.
They must not be done based on potential return on investment
Or likelihood to succeed.
You must gamble on the priorities, the important ones, the ones
Worth sacrificing for the investment.

Pretend it's the end.
Forgiveness is drawn from your spiritual bank account.
You can't bankrupt heaven.
Life rushes to crescendo, the petty arguments are peeled away
From your eyes, as you gaze upon the value of the inner core of
Significance,
What life is all about.

Pretend it's the end.
You will love as if the clock was ticking to a final hour.
You will love as if you will never see your family, friends and
Strangers again.
You will love as if you did not have a life time of second chances
To say all the things you hesitated to say.
You can't remove the bruises your words heaped on the soul
Of an innocent person who stepped off the emotion curb
Into the path of your runaway tongue.

Pretend it's the end
And request the flowers, while you can see and touch and smell.

Ask loved ones to donate to the cancer societies and special
Causes on your behalf,
While you are alive,
Before grateful people are aware of your motivation.
You must call and visit relatives and friends that we don't see
Until weddings, funerals and holidays.
Wouldn't it be nice to trade eulogies and write each other nice
Obituaries while we can read,
Write and hear them.
We can include a recent photograph in our obituary.

Pretend it's the end and show that you love and receive love in
Return.
Pretend it's the end show the world your character, faith, courage
And generosity.

ush me

Push me when I am behind,
Hold me when I sway.
Anchor me in my place
So I won't fly away.

Help me when it's time to leap,
A game of leap frog we will play.
And we will add to the Congo line
As many as we can today.
Pull me when I need to move,
When time is getting late.

Help me as I improve
And I will reciprocate.

To push and pull my neighbor
Will help us both advance,
As we return the favor
We each savor the chance.

Romancing my own

The sun sets.
The sun rises
On beautiful women
Of all makes and sizes.
So many luscious ladies spend
Their evenings alone;
But my emphasis is at home,
Romancing my own.

While jogging on the seashore
To the ovations of the waves;
There can't possibly be more
Temptations to misbehave.
But, my mind is on dancing
With her, on the beach skipping stones.
My mind is in my comfort zone,
Romancing my own.

Just running under the piers
Has caused me to reflect on life.

My royal highness adheres
To me as loyal as a wife
Who knows there's places I won't go,
Not because of fear of the unknown,
But my desire to be home,
Romancing my own.

Too many marriages unravel
From pressures of the lonely nights.
The time apart due to travel
Can heighten the tension and fights.
But, experience has taught me
And absence from my love has shown,
That my thoughts are on home,
Romancing my own.

The sun sets.
The sun rises
On beautiful women
Of all makes and sizes.
So many luscious ladies spend
Their evenings alone;
But my emphasis is at home,
Romancing my own.

Serving Grace

You stood with the serving towel
Draped across your arm,
Prepared to meet a need
That was not your own.
Jesus washed
His disciples feet,
To teach us
So we would repeat
As these acts of service
Are the cornerstone,
Of loving your neighbor.

You served as a volunteer
And released your charm,
Which caught the eye and spirit
Of those around you.
Your pleasant disposition smiled,
And showed that you were reconciled,
Was lost, but found
And the grace of God surrounds you.

So much is expected of you

With promise you were brought into this world
To joyous parents who felt no regrets.
Your relatives praised your birth as you curled
Against your pillow in the bassinet.

We wondered how the world would affect you;
If we were strong enough to raise you right.
We vowed to support and not neglect you;
Protect you from the dangers of the night.

So much is expected of you.
It may overwhelm what you do;
But you are capable of coming through
And brilliantly confirming
What we know to be true.

To school and church and private recitals
Exposure to values we knew would last.
We knew that love and faith would be vital
To strengthen you, when you felt like an outcast.

So much time and love's invested in you.
You were given a lead, now run the race
As one inspired and tested and true
To your potential as you embrace
A mission to live a committed life.

So much is expected of you
You're special beyond what you do.
You've had some breaks,
Made some mistakes,
But the Lord is praying you through
The madness as you look beyond the strife.

So much is expected of you.
It may overwhelm what you do;

But you are capable of coming through
And brilliantly confirming
What we know to be true.

The anniversary song

We harness the harmony,
Years of unbroken communion
And never ending story lines.
We quantified uncertainty
To form a more perfect union;
To form a marriage that defines
Us and aligns us to be strong,
As we sing the anniversary song.

The annual celebration
Elicits moments of reflection,
To insecure times in the past.
When immature conversations
Revealed that love feared rejection,
Because some said it would not last.
We struggled and thought we were wrong,
But we sang the anniversary song.

I feel love's precocious with you.
I feel love's ferocious and due
To always feel reaching for it's prime.
I feel love has curiosity;
Distance over time, velocity

That will keep us fresh, sublime.
And we will laugh and get along
And sing the anniversary song.

The answer is Jesus Christ

The world is an obstacle course
Survival is the obsession.
And people crave a power source
To forgive sins and hear confessions.
The answer is Jesus Christ.

The world is a battle of means
Against those on the lower rungs;
Extremes and people in between
The significant and unsung.
The answer is Jesus Christ.

The nations are preoccupied
With longevity in office;
Priorities at times denied
As criminals feed off justice.
The answer is Jesus Christ.

As violent crimes proliferate
The government increases
The number of jails.
Immoral acts obliterate
The values as more families fail.
The answer is Jesus Christ.

The questions are raised
While we're mourning;
Rhetorical and interrogatives.
Historical facts shout a warning
Choose wisely with our prerogatives;
For the answer is Jesus Christ.

The Babe in the manger

Because He lived,
We should not live as strangers,
But as an extended family of neighbors;
For we are linked to the Babe in the manger.
Oh fingerprint my soul!

To confirm that we have labored
In the same vineyards,
We share a kindred spirit;
We are womb mates, joined at the heart;
Our collective value
Exceeds the sum of our parts.

Because He lived,
We acknowledge that focusing on Him
Can transform.
An arctic heart in winter is warmed;
For the spirit at this time of year
Can flower the frozen tundra,
And melt the icy dispositions
Of despondent faces.

Because He lived,
We are aware of the dangers
That try to diminish our worth.
The Babe in the manger
Taught us that the world
Needs our ideas and contributions.
And though many may say
There's no room in the inn;
We must find a barn, a manger
In our hearts,
To serve as a conduit to bring
His thoughts to life.

The hem of His garment

I have sinned.
I have sinned so much,
My soul is stained beyond recognition.
I have offended
The things I've touched,
Therefore in such
A depraved condition,
God must identify me,
As my next of kin,
From the imprint of my soul,
Which is soiled in sin.

I'm on the fringes,
On the periphery,

Of a life that hinges
On misery.
My family is scattered
My world is torn,
Relationships that mattered
Are battered and worn.
I need to touch
The hem of His garment
With my soul.
The hem of His garment
Will make me whole.

I am incomplete.
The world makes matters worse.
I repeatedly go down in defeat
I am leveled by the curse
Of Adam that's ingrained in me,
As my sin separates me from inner peace.
This same sin is contained in me
As I seek release.

I need to touch
The hem of His garment
With my soul
And let His power
Leave His body
And make me whole.

They're seeking to whom they should pray

They're incomplete and needing
The chance to buy a vowel.
They face defeat and bleeding
But will not throw in the towel.

The hypocrites and sinners
That constantly block their path.
Their ranks aren't getting thinner
Every time they do the math.

They feel forsaken and they are seeking
They're separate and feeling apart.
And weary of judgmental critiquing
Which caused a tightness that stiffened their hearts.

They surfed congregations
Exploring their attention
To pain and obligations
Of seekers in dissension.

They're seeking.
Their on a journey.
If you have directions
Please stop them and say.
In speaking, not as an attorney
Show them to whom they should pray.

Religions are confusing
Competitive in beliefs,
While morally losing
And apathy is the thief.

Everyone has the angle
But the methods they employ
Show values are mangled
For there's an absence of joy.

They're seeking.
They're on a journey.
If you have directions
Please stop them and say.
In speaking, not as an attorney
Show them to whom they should pray.

They want to believe

They want to believe;
While standing in the rain,
Their trousers and sleeves
Drenched from the pain
Of living life.
They want to believe;
In skirts and dresses,
That have seen few successes,
As they are giving life

A chance to repair
Their souls,
If it is fair.

They want to believe;
In greater numbers they gather
Around the church light,
For they wish to experience
The right hand of God,
The healing hand,
To shelter their souls,
As blankets and umbrellas
So they will feel loved
And therefore, understand
His message.

They want to believe;
So they withstand the elements,
To see if God is real, if He is relevant;
To validate the message of salvation.
So they peer through the doors
And watch the congregation.
They want to believe.
They read the pamphlets
And search for satisfaction
As they absorb the sermons
Not of words, but actions.

This old soul

This old soul
Won't get me there
Without a tune-up and some body work.
I need a mechanic to repair
The damage I sustained
In a world full of pain.

The accidents were not all my fault.
Some were random acts, collisions.
A few hit and runs and I was caught
While making poor unwise decisions.

This old soul
Won't make it to heaven
Without an extensive overhaul.
For I have sinned
Seven hundred times seven;
So many times I can't recall.

I ran through red lights and
Warning signs,
Accumulated numerous citations.
And hoping God is not counting fines
As He tallies the violations.

This old soul
Won't get me to heaven
Without an extensive overhaul.

And though I have sinned
Seven hundred times seven
Jesus forgave me
When I answered His call.

Thoughts

Sometimes I lie back on the beach and let the waves come to me,
But when I go out to meet the waves and actually engage the current, I feel more involved. My action is a conversation with the water, a collaboration because I was integral with the process.

The Lord made me cerebral
So I could contemplate on Him
With my mind.
He made my heart His cathedral,
So that I could worship Him
And find
Peace and understanding
As I played hide and seek
With the Comforter.

The Lord made me emotional
So I could seek Him humbly
With my soul.
He made me sociable
So when He comes to me
I can cajole
Others persuasively,
To investigate His love.

To love is my calling

To love is my calling
And I must concede,
To spend time installing
Love to fit His needs.
My sense of purpose
Is tied to His will,
I'm scratching the surface
To bolster my skill.

To love is my calling
As He's teaching me joy.
Love is enthralling
As it reaches me, joy
Enraptures my soul
And sets into motion
And captures my soul
And fuels my devotion.

To love is my calling
I'm honored to say,
That people are falling
Constantly my way.
An eternal sentence
Is what I proclaim.
I feel in repentance
Through the power
Of His name.

To love is my calling
And I must concede,
To spend time installing
Love to fit His needs.
My sense of purpose
Is tied to His will,
I'm scratching the surface
To bolster my skill.

Verona in the garden

As creeping phloxes line the walkway,
The path to your front door explodes in colors,
As fireworks on the fourth of July.
The arbored entrance to the walk
Has sentinels of wrought iron benches
That sit in full view of the bird feeder,
Where finches dine on your hospitality;
Where squirrels extract a gratuity
And demonstrate their ingenuity
And their originality,
As they frolic among
The other members
Of this idyllic orchestra.

Your tender hands upon
The four o' clocks and hollyhocks,
The bleeding hearts and yellow roses.
Your artistic eye make bushes extraordinary

As your touch discloses
The individual forms that vary
From predictable to topiary.
The pampered plants and animals
Grow to magnificent maturity.

The echineacea and day lilies flourish
With daisies and achellea of the pearls
In attendance as skillful hands massage
The seedlings of love nourished
Flora that lie dormant until the wake up call
Whispers upon their petals
And they respond with a barrage
Of beauty as young boys and girls
To doting parents.

Irises and delphiniums
The hyacinths and daffodils
Consort in the millennium
To beautify as each fulfills
The inspiration of your art
As you nurse the blossoms to bloom
In splendor for the world to savor the perfume
From your maternal garden nurtured with love.

You plant the flowers, the bouquets and hues
Adorn the canvass, saturate the air
With fragrant aerosols and wondrous views
Of humble bees and butterflies
And fauna that flaunt
The uniforms of Nature.

At night, the screened in porch attracts the breeze.
The hammock sways invitingly.
The evening torches, the bamboo sleeves
Emits a flame uniting me
With thoughts of you amidst the bird baths
And the fertile fruits of your labor;
The celebrated garden paths
That stir the interest of your neighbors
As they marvel at your garden's invitation
And offer respect through imitation.

Hibiscus and hydrangea are your children.
The humming birds are your offspring;
They are blessed as recipients of your
Maternal instincts.
You walk as the maternal gardener
Among the clematis and hyacinths,
As the rest of the potpourri
Respond with predictable joy,
In appreciation of your passion
And patience with all things beautiful.

We are blessed

We are blessed because of your choice
To serve in the work of the Lord.
We are empowered and rejoice
Refreshed, renewed, restored
As we think of the many ways
To lift you up and give you praise.

We are blessed by your decision
To think of others and their needs;
To work to support the vision;
To help the Church of Christ succeed.
The angels are in formation;
To lead in the celebration.

When Reverend MC Pettie prays

The Reverend humbly took to one knee,
The congregation sat expectantly.
With elbow planted at the edge of thigh,
He went from barely audible to a humble cry,
As he petitioned fervently
For God to hear His servant's plea.
Great God have mercy
Was a recurring phrase.
The church says Amen
When MC Pettie prays.

He said God fixed the heart
And regulated the mind.
He healed the sick
And gave sight to the blind.
Salvation was at our fingertips.
God, the Father wants a relationship
With us to help mend our evil ways
And grant Him glory and give Him the praise.

The church was steamy
MC prayed the good news.
It rocked my heart
As I reeled in the pews.
And perspiration under arms
And hands
Made me think if angels need
Ceiling fans.
Great God have mercy
I can hear his voice raise.
The church says Amen
When MC Pettie prays.

He was a deacon the first time I heard
Him pour out his heart at the throne of grace
I was mesmerized by poetic words
That stirred the spirit and seemed to place
Me vulnerable beneath the Master's gaze
With a repentant heart to change my ways.

I remember once the Deacon started
His prayer by thanking God for answered prayer.
He told of a day when the clouds parted
And he received a message from God where
He was called to a higher level
To help the Master to thwart the devil
And banish him to the fiery deep.
The still small voice said to "Feed My sheep."
He went down a deacon
And one day he heard
The still small voice say to preach the word.

"And Lord when this old life is over
And this old world will be no more.
Present me faultless to your throne in glory
On the other side of Jordan's shore."
Great God have mercy
Remember this phrase
Delights all heaven
When Reverend MC Pettie prays.

When Tonya sings "Precious Lord"

When Tonya sings "Precious Lord"
From the choirstand to the pews;
The people cry, hands in their laps;
Small children wake up from their naps,
To hear her proclaim the Good News.

When Tonya sings "Precious Lord,"
The minds drift to their sinful past;
For the sin soaked congregation,
Are nodding in confirmation,
For through her voice His net was cast.

Her voice aloft on the rafters
Awesomely echoed on the beams;
Ascending from grief to laughter,
Manifesting God is supreme.

His mercy penetrates a soul
And through her instrument of peace

They sensed that He is in control
And they let go
Their sin is released.

When Tonya sings "Precious Lord,"
The heavens are linked to this place,
Her song transports them to His arms,
Free of flames and false alarms,
At rest with soothing words of grace.

When Tonya sings "Precious Lord,"
From the choir stand to the pews;
The people cry, hands in their laps;
Small children wake up from their naps
To hear her proclaim the Good News.

Wherever you go, I will go

Wherever you go I will go.
Where you travel I will trod;
Your people shall be my people
Your God will be my God.

Your customs and language I will learn,
I will be your lover and your friend.
And for services in return
I require love that never ends.

Wherever you go I will go
From Sante Fe to Cape Cod.

I will help us to grow
And your God will be my God.

Where was God?

Where was He when
The storms were raging,
When you struggled
In a sea of strife?

He was there
Actively engaging
The negative forces
That pounded your life.

Where was He when
You were despairing,
Badly battered
From the wages of sin?

He was there
Always present, always caring,
And working miracles
Against the stages of sin.

Where was He when
You tossed in sorrow,
Knocked off balance,
Unable to stand?

He was there
Wading in tomorrow,
Offering His strength to you,
Extending His hand.

Where was He when
Alienation
Was your companion
Against the devil's brigade?

He was there
At your battle station,
Encouraging you
When you were afraid.

Why am I proud of you?

Why am I proud of you?
It's more of who you are
Than what you do;
What you represent
Not what you own;
The fact that I know you,
Not that you are known
By others.

Why am I proud of you?
Good manners and etiquette,
Your substance and depth of feeling;
The simple things you don't forget,

The major things remembered.
The revealing
Conversations that put me at ease;
You are my beloved child
Of whom I am pleased.

Why am I proud of you?
And honored by the affinity
And the prestige allowed
To have you as kin to me;
As a friend to me;
To watch you gather the range
Of experiences;
Knowing that you would rather
Change your plans than harm
Anyone.

Why am I proud of you?
Because you are grounded
In your faith;
Because you are surrounded
With joy and your faith
Does strengthen you
As you model,
Mentor and manage to live
A life that fulfills
Your mission
And glorifies God.

Yes, I say I am a Christian

My interest in the bottom-line
Has caused me to distort the math,
With a tendency to malign
Any obstacle in my path.
And yet, I say I'm a Christian.

I'm on display with selfish acts.
This lack of wisdom counteracts,
The eager souls I could attract,
When people know I'm a Christian.

My neighbor is an after thought
And gossip fills me until I'm caught.
My actions aren't as I was taught,
And yet, I say I'm a Christian.

Prefer the strong, condemn the weak,
Choked with anger until I can't speak,
I seldom turn the other cheek
And yet, I say I'm a Christian.

While traffic slows I'm at my worst
To act in anger is my curse.
I treat my neighbor in reverse,
And yet, I say I'm a Christian.

Jesus conquered death and disease
And asked that we upon our knees,

Would pray and help the least of these;
To show the world that we're Christians.

But when I have a complex day
And little things don't go my way;
I do not close my eyes to pray,
And yet I say I'm a Christian.

I purchase what I can't afford.
I'm kind to garner a reward,
Abuse the temple of the Lord,
And yet, I say I'm a Christian.

I'm work in progress on a bet
That God's not finished with me yet.
His ten commandments I forget,
And yet, I say I'm a Christian.

My inconsistency is met
In a loving and caring way.
His patience issues no regrets
For He forgives me when I stray.
And yes, I say I'm a Christian.

Your end of the bargain

The price has already been paid;
Full value tendered, no discounts.
The sacrifice has been made;
No installments, the full amount.
He covered the margin for you.
Your end of the bargain is not overdue.

You may ask me, whom should you fear?
In your mother womb he appeared
And numbered the hairs on your head;
Inspired you to life and said
You are special, wondrously made;
Fear not, so do not be afraid
For He is God, the only one,
Who sent His only begotten Son
So that His death alone, atones,
Redeems, reclaims, restores His own.

The price has already been paid;
Full value tendered, no discounts.
The sacrifice has been made;
No installments, the full amount.
He covered the margin for you.
Your end of the bargain is not overdue.

In Memorial

*H*e smiled and closed his eyes

(To Sharon Sherbondy on the passing of her father, Bill Brown)

It is a difficult story
That stresses relationship mending;
Involving God in His glory
As He shapes a meaningful ending.
In time, He softened the waters.
In time, He taught to compromise.
The fence between father and daughter
Was gone,
And he smiled and closed his eyes.

The plot defied normal conventions;
No formulas to this gut wrenching tale;
A miracle, divine attention
Is what was needed for love to prevail.
The years brought you close to each other,
When years saw bridges burn in thin air.
This change in fortune pleased your mother,
For heavenly tears wash and repair.

Though family members were torn apart;
Emotional toll roads twist and turn,
As you survey wounds of a broken heart,
You can not linger on the powder burns,
But on the healing that you watched take place.
You may not comprehend, but can surmise,
As you held his hand and looked on his face,

He saw Jesus,
And smiled and closed his eyes.

We are born of blessings, but learn to curse,
When we can't manufacture things as planned.
We keep confessing and learn to rehearse
The script, but don't understand
Why life takes an alternate direction;
We get cloud cover over sunny skies,
But God inspired a course correction
And showed His love,
When your father smiled,
And closed his eyes.

He was always there

(To Angelia Vannoy—in memory of her father,
Deacon Willie Chester Gooden Jr.)

You came into this world
Hitting all the high notes.
Red carpets were unfurled
Not to mention, parades and floats
Said you were welcomed and adored.
The center of attention had arrived.
The surprise package from the Lord
Would set the pace at overdrive.

When you made your first steps,
When you felt the rays of the sun;
When heart broken and you wept,
He made you feel you weren't the only one.
When you fell because of gravity
And winced from the morning glare,
When you made these memories,
He was always there.

When your lungs were developing,
Strong enough for you to breathe,
When you trained your voice to sing,
When you felt the summer breeze.
He was always a constant
As weather and the air.
You can't imagine emptiness,
For he was always there.

When you formed your first sentence,
When you thought you were grown,
When you flexed your independence,
He didn't let you do it alone.
And when you made mistakes
His wisdom was the cornerstone
Of forgiveness that makes
Character and backbone,
The inner strength to go the distance,
For those times when life's not fair.
When you pushed against resistance,
He was always there.

You never thought he'd leave.
Constants should be eternal as the sky;
Rivers run and broken hearts grieve
And mortality means to die.
When you were sustaining
Nicks and bruises, wear and tear.
He taught you many things,
For he was always there.

My prayers to the family of Mike Toupé

My prayers go out to the family,
For they must adjust to the fact
That he is not gone on vacation
Or a business trip;
That he will not be coming home
To equip them for tomorrow,
To replay his day and listen to their stories.

My prayers go out to the family,
For reality has rhythm, and the mechanisms
Sometimes strikes
And chimes for intermission,
But this time it struck
To announce the finality of
An earthly session;
His initial experience above ground.

My prayers go out to the family.
There will be repercussions and complications
That will pull at the strength
That challenges and encourages them
To show that they have found
Energy from his memory.

My prayers go out to the family
As they struggle with the shock;
The cruel truth of the matter,

The interrupted dreams;
The world that was shattered
And must be reassembled
Until it resembles a vision off center;
A hampered vision that must reach 20/20,
For he would have wanted it that way.

Although their bodies shake
And their wills tremble,
Each step will not be taken alone.
He is the shadow in evening,
The blanket on cold nights,
The beacon of hope,
The nourishment for their souls.

He walks beside them
Apologizing for his early departure;
Despondent over not saying good-bye
As he caught the early train to heaven.
He sits in heaven immersed in tears cried
With those who have gone ahead,
For those who are still on the journey.

My heart goes out to the family;
The hearts opened wide
From the surgical incision of death
As life absorbs the essence of love,
They walk around in fear as they reach
For hope in the darkness of uncertainty.

My prayers go out to the family
As they search for explanations
And signs of the inevitable, the if only's;
As they doubt the fairness of life,
Scoff at justice, but rationalize that the Master's plan
Is written in a text we cannot decipher.
They vacillate between the stages of mourning,
Crying, how could this happen without warning,
As they ponder lessons from his demise.
They recreate the clues, retrospective revelations
To open their eyes
To things they could have done differently,
In an effort to embrace blame
They evaluate doing or not doing, knowing or not knowing;
Things they should have added or things to replace.
They seek memories to live by and nightmares to erase.

My heart goes out to the family.
How would he want them to act?
How would he want them to handle the fact
That he is not coming home to them,
But waits for the day when they will come
To their new residence and live without fear
Of separation.

Each life teaches us,
Each life reaches us
And grabs us at the core of our being,
Each life touches us
And it clutches us
By our souls and begs us to pay attention.

For through seeing the greatness in others
And sharing their special gifts,
We are inspired to reach our potential.
We run as fast and far as our gifts will take us;
Soar as high as wings of talent differentiates us.
As we study excellence and the pursuit
Of standards that validate,
We justify our rung on the ladder.
The harsh reality is that we have to prove ourselves.
We enforce discipline.
We can't succumb to the sadder side
Of issues for they makes us angry and madder inside
Which can breach our concentration.
Time is valuable
As each minute marks our place in line.

My heart goes out to the family.
Life places them on the journey
Afloat, adrift in a raft
Surrounded by loved ones
As they perfect their craft,
They watch others as they play out
Their love ethic and work ethic,
Knowing he is watching.
They study God
As He teaches them to row.
They consciously and innately
Take notes on their position
And how they manage the climate
And the changes in the tide.

My heart goes out to the family.
May they find comfort in his memory,
Instruction from his life
And faith from his source of inspiration.

(Mike Toupé was by profession a product manager in the marketing department of a pharmaceutical company. He died at a young age, leaving behind a wife and young children. Mike was extremely articulate, a hard worker who was dedicated to excellence and high achievement.)

Reflections on a life

I didn't know him well;
Our paths would seldom cross,
But the magnitude of his loss
Cascaded from a heavenly cry
That struck the heart and each eye
Responded with a flow of tears.

I didn't know him well;
We shared in small talk at meetings.
He was cordial in his greetings.
His peers viewed him as strong and wise,
A family man who exercised
With a drive that defied his years.

I know he started before me
And departed before me

In the company.
A quiet man, unassuming,
Someone the master was grooming.
This father, leader, pioneer,
Blessed many lives when he was here,
Personally and in their private lives
And public careers.

I didn't know him well.
I saw his light.
I heard his bell.
We were ships passing in the night,
Who shared respect and shared the light.
I can not say he learned from me,
But I learned from him and eternity
Gives memories as souvenirs.

I didn't know him well;
Our paths would seldom cross,
But friends were shaken by the loss
Of such an upright decent man,
Who touched their lives and taught you can
Enjoy life and the great outdoors
And grow deeply in relationships
As one explores.

(Jay Gardner was a managerial peer of mine for a number of years.
We spent time together at meetings and frequently in the exercise
room. He was an exercise enthusiast and a devoted family man.)

She meant so much to you

(To Lafonda Berry
On the death of her grandmother, Martha Tarver)

She meant so much to you;
The heart at half mast
Listens as taps plays in the background;
As Mahalia sings "Precious Lord."
She meant so much to you;
The memories fast backwards,
As a funeral procession,
Decorated with floats
Of the good and bad times;
Celebrating her life.

She meant so much to you:
A heart broken is a sign of reverence;
Tears of confession
Are a sign of regret,
Apologizing for not being there
Or not being there more.
She meant so much to you,
So you are not concerned with form or fashion;
The make-up runs, being chased
And pushed by the tears
Of separation.

She meant so much to you,
And you wish to tell her

And show her the extent of your caring,
So she could count the ways and weight
Of your indebtedness.
You want her to hear you
And smile, content that your love
Was genuine and complete.

She meant so much to you,
That moments of silence.
Are insufficient;
The moans have meaning.
This is not the time for being polite and proper.
The wailing and the cries of despair
Are the blues for you
And the spirituals of your heart.

She meant so much to you,
And she is proud of who you are
And who you are becoming.
She knows you are her greatest joy.
She knows your heart and watching
The impact of your life on others as you
Continue living the things she taught you,
Will be her greatest joy in heaven.

(LaFonda Berry is a sales representative for the company where I work. She was raised by her grandmother and frequently discussed the impact of her grandmother on her life.)

Trilogy to Melanie B. Stokes

Lord, help us comprehend

Lord help us comprehend,
Why a life so special had to end?
Why a gentle spirit had to ascend
To your personal garden in Heaven?

Lord, help us explain to others;
To little children, when pain smothers
Our hearts and strangles the breath,
As relatives and mothers
Wring their hands and
Shakes their fists at death.

Lord, help us comprehend,
Why suffering comes and why you send
The Comforter?
Why is He dispatched?
How is He superbly matched
To our level of pain,
To our level of need.

Father, we know your will is exquisite,
But we would prefer,
That we did not need
His visit.

Lord, help us comprehend,
Why you needed our loving friend?

If her departure was premature,
If you had no say in the matter,
Help us to endure the questions,
As we engage the doubt.
Father, help us to sort it out.

$\mathcal{A}$ life of significance

She lived a life of significance
And granted wishes.
She was the motor blade
That churned the waters
And made things happen.
She moved in many circles,
Wore many hats, played many roles.
She was the servant to her Lord,
A servant to her people,
A wife, a trusted friend
And loving daughter.

She reached down and pulled
Others up to her side.
She didn't speak down to you
As she changed your elevation.
She was thoughtfulness.
She showed appreciation
For acts of kindness.
She tapped into your wavelength
And communed with you on your frequency.

She cared about you frequently.
She was not infatuated with fame and glory.
When she was there for you,
It was your story that had top billing.

She was not larger than life,
And that was her goal.
She wanted to be at your height,
To look you in the eyes of your soul,
To help you gain wisdom and insight,
Thus giving you power to be in control.
She was not a heavy weight,
But was strong enough to lift your spirits.

She lived a life of significance
And her death will change lives,
And alter the world, positively.
Her death will follow the pattern of her life
And contribute and make a difference.
Her smile will always be remembered;
Her gentle ways,
The unselfish rays of her light
Will be immortal and flow
Through many generations.

I had the honor of standing in her light,
Immersed in the healing rays
Of positive expectations.
I sat at her feet with the other students,
As she instructed through a life
That was a demonstration

Of love and motivation,
Our responsibility,
Our obligation,
To live a life consistent
With the will of the Author
Of all creation.

The color red is grieving

The color red is grieving,
In a stream of crimson tears.
Compassion and Love are weaving
A quilt to illustrate the years
And acts of kindness, she displayed
To friends whose hearts were bleeding.
When bad things happened and
Others left, she stayed
Supporting them and leading
Them to a comfortable place,
Where God would bless them with His grace.

The eyes of Fashion, Etiquette
And Elegance are weeping,
For she enhanced them as she set
The standard for safe keeping.
She organized and planned affairs,
That showed more than a touch of class,
But broad brush strokes,
Artistic flairs
Of creativity, unsurpassed

And strangers are sobbing with those
Who knew her best,
For they can sense
The beauty that is unopposed,
As pictured in the evidence.
Her laugh was genuine, true;
Unselfish assistance to issues
Was her trademark, as she applied
Tenderness to wounded pride;
Her beauty external
Matched her beauty inside.

The color red is grieving,
In a stream of crimson tears;
Reticent and unbelieving,
But thankful for the years
Of unspeakable joy.

(Melanie B. Stokes was a dear friend, a compassionate and inspiring individual. She had achieved her storybook lifestyle which she so richly deserved. She took her own life while suffering from postpartum psychosis. She is deeply missed and fondly remembered.)

Trilogy to Idella Tines

Dinner with the King of Kings

Mama, Sister, Idella Tines,
Her life was her ticket to glory;
Her invitation to dine
With the King of Kings;
To see the Master
And tell her story,
In the company of angels,
As she tries on her wings.

Her love for Jesus
Earned the invitation,
Her gentle spirit
Led her to paradise.
She was the quiet queen
Of the plantation.
She was the self less one,
Who willingly paid the price,
By putting children first,
Through endless sacrifice.

Four score and seventeen
Years upon this earth.
Two score and fifteen
Years in married life.
To sixteen children
She gave birth.

She was Dock's companion,
His loyal and loving wife.
God told them to be fruitful
And they multiplied,
He told her to be steadfast
And she assumed many roles.
In return He gave her honor
And dignity and enriched her soul.

She made homemade ice cream
On Sundays after church.
And showed kindness to strangers.
And when family members were lost,
She led the search
To rescue them from danger.

She helped lead the family through
Hard times and tribulations;
From the early days
Of the Clarksdale migration
To the present,
She was at the center,
Always giving her best.
She was a rock,
A trusting foundation
For nearly a hundred winters.
For nearly a hundred Springs,
She labored in the vineyard,
But now she must rest,
And greet her friends and ancestors
And dine with the King of Kings.

Mother, seamstress, loving wife

When the fabric of family was frayed,
She stitched the tears, repaired the seams.
When courage escaped and some were afraid,
She double stitched to strengthen their dreams.
And when they didn't get the breaks,
She led them to their knees and prayed.
And when they often made mistakes
And others left, she listened and stayed.

Her hands touched the garden
And the flowers grew;
Her hands touched the fabric
And it became a quilt.
Her hands touched a shoulder
And instantly you knew,
She was there for you.
She was not there to judge
Or remind you of your guilt.

She is gone and the empty sensations
Must be filled by the values she planted.
For she touched and spanned six generations
And in her lifetime she was granted
The privilege to lead a meaningful life,
As mother, seamstress and loving wife.

A tribute to Sister

I have seen the spring from which you drank,
And nourished your values and formed your
Creativity.
I have walked along the river bank
Where you were suckled in nativity;
Where your tears were diluted
And your dreams were rooted,
In soil that was rich and demanding.

Sister was the mist that cooled your brow
And soaked your limbs;
The liniment that massaged where you ached.
She was the river that led you to Him,
The one who gives the peace
That passes understanding.

I have seen the tree that provided shade
From the heat of life's journey;
That gave lemons for lemonade;
That you leaned against
To gain your balance;
And to hide behind
When you were afraid.

We knew the end was coming.
We could hear the drumming
In the distance getting closer,
At a faster rate.

But we did not wish to think that fate
Would be punctual
And honor her expiration date.

(My grandmother, Idella Tines was the matriarch, the spiritual leader
of the family, who lived a very blessed life which will touch generations upon generations until the end of time.)

We lived through his life:
A tribute to Walter Payton

We lived through his life;
We were grounded in his greatness,
He did not short circuit his fame,
He used it to electrify a city
By the way he played the game.

He was precision.
He stopped on a dime, reversed his field,
An artist, a maestro with flair.
Behind a wall, a human shield
He left defenders grasping for air.

He was elusive.
Evasive runs with ballet moves,
He faced Goliaths unafraid.
When he struck the ground
His strength renewed,
A somersault, a touchdown made.

We lived through his life,
To give as much on a loss or gain
As on a breakaway run;
Acknowledge team mates
And play through pain
And finish strongly what is begun.

The standards he set to emulate;
That championship effort must come first.
The memories as footage will stimulate
The passion to succeed and quench the thirst.
He taught us in struggles not to yield
Unless the best effort was on the field.

His conduct was with dignity and grace.
He was loved by many, admired by peers.
He stared adversity in the face
And gave us hope to conquer the fears
And we in tribute
Release the tears.

He was a fan of life
With a plan for life;
A humble player on the squad.
He shared with family and friends.
Devoted father to his children;
Companion to his wife;
A servant to his God.

We lived through his life.
We grieve in his death.

We dedicate moments of silence
And celebrate each breath,
For we will miss his presence
And are thankful for the latitude
To express in effervescence
Our collective gratitude;
For he showed us that life could be fun
And beautiful and the long runs
With those you love
Make it all worthwhile.
We love you "Sweetness, Number 34."

Wilt & Dale, Sweetness & Payne

Abbreviated lives, major losses;
As gladiators, they bowed to the cheers of their fans.
But all is silent, the checkered flag is at half mast
As each man crosses
The finish line,
Awash in the tears of their fans.

They had dominion over their sport;
Spectators marveled at each victory.
Folks shared opinions and vowed to support
Each man's induction into history.
They were heroes on the track, on the fields
And on the courses.
Their lust for life and energy appealed
To hungry spirits and excellence endorses
Their brand of passion and the way

They played their games,
As they excelled to levels few will attain.
We learned to celebrate fame,
And lived through the lives of
Wilt and Dale, Sweetness and Payne.

The trophy cases of our hearts are filled
With memories of watching them train.
To think their fluid motions have been stilled
Is tragic, although their magic remains
A monument to remember and retain,
As reverent thoughts of
Wilt and Dale, Sweetness and Payne.

Departure from this earth was premature;
Fruit picked before the harvest, in their prime.
We learned to say I love you more often
For we're not sure, how much time is left
To say goodbye to those we love,
Since we're all running out of time.

We stood on the sidelines, in the bleachers
On the track and in the galleys,
And applauded as their talents grew.
As leaders, their actions were modeled
From the mountains to the valleys
From the courses to the alleys
As we emulated their ways,

They stimulated our days
And we knew,

They taught us to concentrate,
And at high speeds;
To use instinct to break away and free
Ourselves to take risks and fill the need
To add excitement to life and to be
Enriched as they were, when they entertained
Us, before the emptiness, before the void.
Death will not diminish the magic
Nor will the magic be destroyed;
For through their loss there are major gains.
We commemorate,
Wilt and Dale, Sweetness and Payne.

(Wilt Chamberlin, Dale Earnhardt, Walter Payton and Payne Stewart
were legends in their field who were adored by millions.)

About the Author

Orlando Ceaser is a Sales Director for a major pharmaceutical company. He uses his communication skills to lead, inspire and motivate people to reach for their potential.

He has held leadership positions in his profession and within the church. He was a Deacon, Sunday school teacher, Superintendent of Sunday School and a member of various committees. He is currently on the Drama team and Careers ministries at WillowCreek Community Church in South Barrington, Illinois.

He is the author of *Teach the Children to Dance* and *Leadership —Above the Rim*. In addition to his volumes of poetry, he has written several articles on leadership and motivation.

His activities include writing, public speaking, drama, career counseling and running.

He resides in South Barrington, Illinois with his wife Verona and two children, Veronica and Brian.

Notes

Notes

Notes